To: DEIR
From. LeRAY TATE
4/3/74

HOW DOES THE WIND BLOW?

An I WONDER WHY Reader

HOLT, RINEHART AND WINSTON, INC.

New York   Toronto   London   Sydney

HOW DOES THE WIND BLOW?

By LAWRENCE F. LOWERY

Consultant, ABRAHAM S. FISCHLER

Illustrated by BETTY FRASER

Copyright © 1969 by Holt, Rinehart and Winston, Inc.
All Rights Reserved
Printed in the United States of America

Library of Congress Catalog Card Number: 69-20256
03-081171-6

90123 52 987654321

Air is almost everywhere.
It is all around you.
Cup your hands,
and the air fills them.

Air is in all the houses.
It is in all the shops.
Air is on top of the highest
mountains.
It is down in the deepest caves.

Air is in you, too.

Air is almost everywhere,
but no one has ever seen it!
It has no color.
It has no smell.
You can not taste it, not even if you try.

Even so, you can learn about the air.
You can begin by watching things
that are moved by air.

Air that moves is called wind.

Sometimes the wind blows slowly.
Sometimes it blows very fast.
Sometimes there is no wind at all.

When there is no wind,
the smoke from chimneys
rises straight up toward the sky.
Leaves hanging on the trees
do not move.
Papers stay where they are
and do not fly about.

The air is very still.

On other days, you can feel the wind
blowing softly against your face.
A light breeze is the name for air
that moves slowly.

In a light breeze, leaves rustle
with a soft, gentle sound.
Smoke drifts wherever
the light breeze may send it.

Sometimes the air moves a bit faster.
It moves fast enough to bend
small twigs on trees and bushes.
It shakes and stirs the leaves.

Air that moves this fast is called
a gentle breeze.

In a gentle breeze, small flags flutter.
They may even stand out straight
as they wave.

Have you ever felt a gentle breeze
when you played in the open air?

A wind is not always light.
A wind is not always gentle.
Sometimes it is strong enough
to blow small papers to and fro.
A wind this strong is called
a moderate wind.

It is a wind that blows a little bit harder
than a gentle breeze.

In a moderate wind, small branches
move this way and that.
They rub softly against each other.
You can hear them
if you stand nearby and listen.

On some days, the wind blows so hard that small trees sway back and forth. Leaves seem to whisper as they brush against one another.

A wind that blows this hard is called a fresh wind.

A fresh wind can blow across the water.
It puts curly white tops on the waves.
The little whitecaps dance on the water
in this kind of wind.

Sometimes air moves still more quickly.
It shakes the large branches of trees.
It blows off hats and makes your
kite fly high.

No wonder a wind like this is called
a strong wind!

A strong wind hums and sings
as it blows through telephone wires.
It makes the rain beat hard against
the windows.
It pulls at your umbrella and turns it
inside out.

Sometimes a wind blows so hard
that it makes tall trees bend.
It breaks off twigs.
It blows down signs.
It smashes windows.

A wind that blows so hard
is called a gale.

A gale can break large branches
from a tree. It can blow down
trees that stand in its way.

Have you ever tried to walk
against this kind of wind?
Walking can be hard on such
a windy day.

The wind can grow still stronger!
It can blow harder and faster
than a gale.
It can blow the ocean into giant waves.

It can toss a big boat onto the shore.
It can blow down street lights,
or tear a building apart.

A wind that blows this strongly
is called a hurricane.

A hurricane comes with great loud roars. Safe inside your house, you can hear the wind rushing on its way. Home is the place to be until the hurricane passes by.

There is another wind that is
still stronger and more dangerous.
It is the wind that sounds louder
than a fleet of jets roaring by.
It is a wind that can lift houses
and animals and trees into the air.
It can even lift a railroad car and
smash it to the ground.

A wind like this is called a tornado.

The air in a tornado spins like a top.
As it spins, it picks up dust and dirt
that makes it look very dark.
This dark, spinning tornado does not stay
in one place very long.
It moves across the land.
A tornado can do much damage
before it stops.

Moving air can be many things.
It can rush about like an angry giant
in a terrible hurricane.
Or it can spin through little towns
in a roaring tornado.

But moving air can be the quiet breeze
that cools us on a summer's day.
It can be the breeze that blows
our boats across a pond.
It can be the wind that whirls
autumn leaves from trees.

Moving air can do many good things.
Moving air can do many bad things.
But most of the time, moving air
seems to be as gentle as a breeze.